Cracking the Affiliate Code Insider Secrets for Marketing Success

Vincent

Copyright © [2023]

Title: Cracking the Affiliate Code Insider Secrets for Marketing Success
Author's: Vincent

This book was printed and published by [Publisher's: **Vincent**] in [2023]

ISBN:

TABLE OF CONTENT

Chapter 1: Introduction to Affiliate
Marketing   07

What is Affiliate Marketing?

History and Evolution of Affiliate Marketing

Benefits of Affiliate Marketing

Chapter 2: Getting Started with Affiliate
Marketing   13

Setting Up Your Affiliate Marketing Strategy

Choosing the Right Affiliate Network

Researching and Selecting Profitable Niches

Finding High-Converting Affiliate Products

Chapter 3: Building a Strong Affiliate
Network   21

Attracting and Recruiting Affiliates

Developing Relationships with Affiliates

Providing Affiliate Support and Resources

Chapter 4: Creating Successful Affiliate Marketing Campaigns   27

Crafting Compelling Affiliate Offers

Designing Effective Landing Pages

Implementing Conversion Optimization Techniques

Utilizing Persuasive Copywriting Strategies

Chapter 5: Maximizing Affiliate Marketing Revenue   35

Implementing Effective Traffic Generation Methods

Leveraging Social Media for Affiliate Marketing Success

Harnessing the Power of Email Marketing

Exploring Advanced Affiliate Marketing Techniques

Chapter 6: Analytics and Tracking for Affiliate Marketing   43

Understanding Key Performance Indicators (KPIs)

Tracking Affiliate Performance and Conversions

Analyzing Data to Optimize Campaigns

Chapter 7: Compliance and Legal Considerations in Affiliate Marketing 49

Adhering to FTC Guidelines

Understanding Affiliate Disclosure Requirements

Navigating International Affiliate Marketing Laws

Chapter 8: Scaling and Growing Your Affiliate Business 55

Strategies for Scaling Affiliate Campaigns

Expanding Your Affiliate Network

Diversifying Revenue Streams in Affiliate Marketing

Chapter 9: Overcoming Challenges in Affiliate Marketing 62

Dealing with Affiliate Fraud and Scams

Managing Competition in the Affiliate Space

Staying Updated with Industry Changes and Trends

Chapter 10: The Future of Affiliate Marketing   68

The Evolution of Affiliate Marketing Technology

Predictions and Trends for the Affiliate Marketing Industry

Embracing Innovation for Continued Success

Chapter 11: Conclusion and Action Steps   74

Recap of Key Affiliate Marketing Strategies

Next Steps for Affiliate Marketing Success

Final Thoughts and Encouragement for Marketing Triumph

Chapter 1: Introduction to Affiliate Marketing

What is Affiliate Marketing?

Affiliate marketing is a dynamic and highly lucrative marketing strategy that has gained immense popularity in recent years. In the digital era, it has become a go-to method for businesses to expand their reach and generate substantial revenue. If you are a marketer or have an interest in affiliate marketing, this subchapter aims to provide you with a comprehensive understanding of what affiliate marketing entails.

At its core, affiliate marketing is a performance-based marketing model where businesses reward affiliates for bringing them customers or driving desired actions. These affiliates, often individuals or other businesses, promote products or services through various marketing channels, such as websites, blogs, social media, email marketing, and more. When a customer makes a purchase or completes a specific action, the affiliate earns a commission or receives a predetermined payment.

One of the key advantages of affiliate marketing is its ability to create a win-win situation for both businesses and affiliates. For businesses, affiliate marketing allows them to expand their customer base without investing heavily in advertising or marketing efforts. Instead, they only pay affiliates when they achieve desired results. On the other hand, affiliates benefit from the opportunity to monetize their online presence and earn passive income by promoting products or services they believe in.

To succeed in affiliate marketing, it is essential to understand the various parties involved. The three main players in this ecosystem are the merchant, the affiliate, and the customer. The merchant is the business or brand that offers products or services for promotion. The affiliate is the marketer who promotes these products or service through their marketing channels. Finally, the customer is the end user who makes a purchase or completes an action, thereby generatin revenue for both the merchant and the affiliate.

Affiliate marketing also operates on a unique tracking and attributior system. Affiliates are assigned unique tracking links or codes tha enable businesses to identify which affiliate was responsible fo generating a sale or action. This tracking mechanism ensures accurate commission payouts and provides valuable data for assessing the success of marketing campaigns.

In conclusion, affiliate marketing is an effective and mutually beneficial marketing strategy that allows businesses to expand thei reach and affiliates to earn passive income. By leveraging the power o technology and the internet, affiliates have the opportunity to promote products or services they genuinely believe in, while businesses can tap into a vast network of marketers to increase their sales and revenue Understanding the fundamentals of affiliate marketing is crucial for marketers looking to excel in this niche and unlock the secrets of marketing success.

History and Evolution of Affiliate Marketing

Affiliate marketing has become a prominent and lucrative industry in the field of marketing. In this subchapter, we will delve into the fascinating history and evolution of affiliate marketing, tracing its roots and milestones that have shaped it into what it is today.

Affiliate marketing can be traced back to the mid-1990s when the concept of revenue sharing emerged. The pioneer in this space was Jeff Bezos, the founder of Amazon.com. In 1996, Amazon launched the Amazon Associates program, allowing website owners to earn a commission by promoting Amazon's products. This program laid the foundation for affiliate marketing and set the stage for its exponential growth.

In the early years, affiliate marketing primarily revolved around traditional banner ads and simple text links. However, with the advent of new technologies and the rise of e-commerce, the landscape of affiliate marketing underwent significant changes. The introduction of cookies in the late 1990s allowed merchants to track the source of referrals, enabling more accurate tracking of sales and commissions.

The new millennium brought further advancements, with affiliate networks emerging as a crucial player in the industry. These networks acted as intermediaries, connecting merchants with affiliate marketers and providing a platform for tracking and managing affiliate programs. Commission Junction, founded in 1998, was one of the first affiliate networks to revolutionize the industry and paved the way for numerous others to follow suit.

As the internet continued to evolve, so did affiliate marketing. With the rise of search engines and social media platforms, affiliate marketers found new avenues to reach their target audience. Search engine optimization (SEO) techniques became crucial for driving organic traffic, while social media platforms provided a powerful medium for promoting products and engaging with potential customers.

In recent years, the affiliate marketing landscape has witnessed the emergence of influencers and content creators. These individuals leverage their online presence and credibility to endorse products and generate sales. This form of affiliate marketing has gained immense popularity, especially in niches such as beauty, fashion, and lifestyle.

The evolution of affiliate marketing has been driven by various factors including advancements in technology, changes in consumer behavior, and the growing importance of digital marketing. Today affiliate marketing has become a multi-billion-dollar industry, offering a vast array of opportunities for marketers and businesses alike.

As we delve deeper into this book, we will uncover the insider secrets and strategies that can unlock the full potential of affiliate marketing By understanding its rich history and evolution, we can gain valuable insights into the industry and maximize our success as affiliate marketers.

Benefits of Affiliate Marketing

Affiliate marketing has emerged as a powerful tool in the world of digital marketing, providing numerous benefits for both marketers and businesses. This subchapter will delve into the various advantages of affiliate marketing, offering valuable insights into why it has become an essential strategy for businesses of all sizes and niches.

One of the primary benefits of affiliate marketing is its cost-effectiveness. Unlike traditional marketing methods that often require substantial upfront investments, affiliate marketing allows businesses to pay only for the results they achieve. Marketers are only compensated when their efforts result in a successful sale or lead, making it a highly efficient and budget-friendly option.

Furthermore, affiliate marketing allows businesses to tap into a vast network of marketers who are incentivized to promote their products or services. This creates a win-win situation, as marketers can earn attractive commissions while businesses can reach a wider audience without the need for extensive marketing campaigns. With the right affiliates, businesses can significantly increase their brand visibility and drive more traffic to their websites.

Another significant advantage of affiliate marketing is its ability to drive targeted traffic to a business's website. Affiliates typically have a niche focus, allowing them to attract an audience that is genuinely interested in the products or services being promoted. This results in higher conversion rates and a greater likelihood of generating sales. By leveraging the expertise of affiliates, businesses can effectively reach their target market and increase their chances of success.

Additionally, affiliate marketing offers businesses the opportunity to expand their reach globally. With affiliates located in different regions and markets, businesses can tap into diverse customer segments that may have otherwise been inaccessible. This enables businesses to scale their operations and enter new markets without the need for extensive market research or infrastructure setup.

Lastly, affiliate marketing provides businesses with valuable insights and data that can inform their marketing strategies. By tracking affiliate performance and analyzing consumer behavior, businesses can gain a deeper understanding of their target audience, identify trends, and refine their marketing efforts accordingly. This data-driven approach allows businesses to optimize their campaigns and maximize their return on investment.

In conclusion, affiliate marketing offers a multitude of benefits for marketers and businesses alike. Its cost-effectiveness, ability to drive targeted traffic, global reach, and data-driven approach make it an indispensable tool in the world of marketing. By incorporating affiliate marketing strategies, businesses can enhance their brand visibility, increase their sales, and ultimately achieve long-term marketing success.

Chapter 2: Getting Started with Affiliate Marketing

Setting Up Your Affiliate Marketing Strategy

Affiliate marketing has emerged as one of the most lucrative and popular forms of online marketing. With the potential to generate passive income and reach a wide audience, it is no wonder that many marketers are turning to affiliate marketing as a means to expand their business. However, in order to succeed in this competitive field, setting up a solid affiliate marketing strategy is crucial.

The first step in setting up your affiliate marketing strategy is to clearly define your goals. What do you hope to achieve through affiliate marketing? Are you looking to increase brand awareness, drive traffic to your website, or generate sales? By setting specific and measurable goals, you can tailor your strategy accordingly and track your progress along the way.

Once you have determined your goals, the next step is to identify your target audience. Who are the people most likely to be interested in your products or services? Conduct market research to understand their needs, preferences, and purchasing habits. By understanding your target audience, you can select affiliate programs and partners that align with their interests, increasing the chances of attracting quality traffic and conversions.

Choosing the right affiliate programs and partners is another crucial aspect of your strategy. Look for programs that offer products or services relevant to your niche. Consider factors such as commission rates, cookie duration, and reputation of the affiliate program. Additionally, research potential partners to ensure they have a strong online presence and align with your brand values.

To maximize the effectiveness of your affiliate marketing strategy, it is important to create compelling and engaging content. Whether it is through blog posts, social media posts, or videos, provide valuable information and showcase the benefits of the products or services you are promoting. Incorporate persuasive call-to-actions to encourage your audience to take action and make a purchase.

Monitoring and analyzing your affiliate marketing efforts is essential for optimizing your strategy. Use analytics tools to track key metrics such as click-through rates, conversion rates, and average order value. By analyzing this data, you can identify what is working well and make adjustments to improve your results.

In conclusion, setting up an effective affiliate marketing strategy requires careful planning and execution. By clearly defining your goals, understanding your target audience, selecting the right affiliate programs and partners, creating compelling content, and monitoring your efforts, you can increase your chances of success in the competitive world of affiliate marketing. So, get ready to crack the affiliate code and unlock the secrets to marketing success.

Choosing the Right Affiliate Network

When it comes to succeeding in the world of affiliate marketing, choosing the right affiliate network is crucial. With countless options available, it can be overwhelming to determine which network will best suit your marketing goals and niche. In this subchapter, we will explore the key factors to consider when selecting an affiliate network, ensuring your marketing success.

Firstly, it is essential to understand your target audience and niche. Different affiliate networks cater to specific industries and markets. Therefore, identifying your niche and finding a network that specializes in that area will increase your chances of generating higher conversions and revenue. Conduct thorough research to identify the networks that have a strong presence in your niche and align with your marketing objectives.

Furthermore, consider the reputation and credibility of the affiliate network. It is vital to partner with a network that has a proven track record of success and a solid reputation within the affiliate marketing community. Look for networks that have been in operation for a significant period and have a portfolio of reputable advertisers and publishers. This will ensure that you are working with a trustworthy network that can provide you with the necessary support and resources.

Additionally, evaluate the commission structure and payment terms offered by the affiliate network. Different networks have varying commission rates and payment schedules. Analyze the commission rates in relation to your niche and compare them with other networks. Additionally, consider the payment terms, such as the frequency of payments and the minimum payout thresholds. Selecting a network

that offers favorable commission rates and flexible payment terms wi.
optimize your earning potential.

Moreover, examine the tools and resources provided by the affiliat
network. A robust network should offer a range of tools and resource
to assist you in optimizing your marketing campaigns. Look fo
features such as tracking and reporting tools, creative assets, anc
dedicated affiliate support. These resources will enable you to monito
your performance, create compelling content, and troubleshoot any
issues that may arise.

Finally, consider the network's policies and terms of service. Ensure
that the network's policies align with your marketing strategies anc
ethics. Review the terms and conditions, including the exclusivity
clauses, cookie durations, and promotional methods allowed. By
selecting a network with favorable policies, you can avoid potentia
conflicts and restrictions that may hinder your marketing efforts.

In conclusion, choosing the right affiliate network is crucial for
marketing success in the affiliate marketing niche. By considering
factors such as niche specialization, reputation, commission structure,
provided tools and resources, and network policies, you can make an
informed decision that aligns with your marketing goals. Remember,
the right network will not only enhance your earning potential but also
provide you with the support and resources necessary to thrive in the
competitive world of affiliate marketing.

Researching and Selecting Profitable Niches

In the ever-evolving world of affiliate marketing, one crucial aspect that can make or break your success is selecting the right niche. Identifying a profitable niche is like finding a hidden treasure trove that can provide you with a steady stream of income for years to come. However, with countless niches available, it can be overwhelming to narrow down your options. This subchapter will guide you through the process of researching and selecting profitable niches for your affiliate marketing endeavors.

The first step in this journey is thorough research. Begin by identifying your target audience and understanding their needs, desires, and pain points. Conducting market research, analyzing trends, and studying consumer behavior will provide valuable insights into potential niches. Look for niches that have a substantial audience and offer products or services with high demand.

Keyword research plays a vital role in determining the profitability of a niche. Utilize keyword research tools to identify popular search terms related to your potential niches. Look for keywords with a significant search volume and relatively low competition. This will help you gauge the level of interest in a specific niche and determine the likelihood of ranking well in search engine results.

Another important factor to consider is the level of competition within a niche. While a competitive niche indicates a high demand, it also means that you will face stiff competition from other affiliates. Balancing competition with profitability is key. Consider niches with moderate competition that still offer ample opportunities for growth and profit.

Affiliate networks and programs can be excellent resources for finding profitable niches. Research different affiliate networks and identify those that align with your interests and goals. Explore the available programs within those networks and evaluate their commission rates, conversion rates, and product offerings. Look for niches that have a wide variety of quality products or services to promote, ensuring a greater chance of success.

Lastly, consider your own interests and expertise. Choose a niche that aligns with your passions, as this will make the process more enjoyable and sustainable. Your knowledge and enthusiasm will shine through your marketing efforts and resonate with your audience.

In summary, researching and selecting profitable niches is a crucial step towards affiliate marketing success. Thoroughly research your target audience, conduct keyword research, evaluate competition levels, and explore affiliate networks and programs. By considering these factors and aligning them with your own interests, you can crack the code to finding profitable niches that will set you on the path to marketing success.

inding High-Converting Affiliate Products

n the ever-evolving world of affiliate marketing, the key to success lies n finding high-converting affiliate products. These are products that ot only resonate with your target audience but also generate ubstantial revenue for you as a marketer. However, with countless roducts available in the market, it can be a daunting task to identify he ones that will yield the best results. This subchapter aims to rovide you with invaluable insights and strategies to help you avigate this process and discover high-converting affiliate products.

)ne of the first steps in finding high-converting affiliate products is to nderstand your target audience and their needs. Conduct thorough narket research and analyze the demographics, preferences, and pain oints of your potential customers. This knowledge will enable you to elect products that align with their interests and offer solutions to heir problems. By doing so, you increase the likelihood of generating igher conversions.

Additionally, it is crucial to assess the reputation and credibility of the ffiliate products you consider promoting. Look for products from eputable vendors with a proven track record of delivering quality and :ustomer satisfaction. This will not only enhance your credibility as a narketer but also instill trust in your audience, increasing the ikelihood of conversions.

Furthermore, keep an eye on market trends and emerging niches. Staying updated with the latest developments in your industry will allow you to identify new products with high-conversion potential. By being an early adopter of such products, you can tap into a less competitive market and gain a competitive advantage.

Another effective approach to finding high-converting affiliat products is to leverage affiliate networks and marketplaces. Thes platforms bring together a wide range of products from variou vendors, making it easier for marketers to discover and compar different options. They often provide valuable insights, such a conversion rates, commission rates, and affiliate tools, which can assis you in making informed decisions.

Lastly, consider testing and tracking the performance of differen affiliate products. Implementing split testing and closely monitorin metrics like conversion rates, click-through rates, and earnings pe click can provide valuable data-driven insights. Continuously optimiz your marketing strategies based on the results obtained, thereb maximizing conversions and profitability.

By employing these strategies and adopting a data-driven approach you can effectively navigate the affiliate marketing landscape and finc high-converting affiliate products. Remember, success in affiliat marketing lies not only in selecting the right products but also ir understanding and connecting with your target audience. Cracking the code to finding high-converting affiliate products will undoubtedl) pave the way for your marketing success.

Chapter 3: Building a Strong Affiliate Network

Attracting and Recruiting Affiliates

Affiliate marketing is a powerful strategy that allows businesses to tap into a vast network of individuals who promote their products or services in exchange for a commission. However, for this marketing technique to be successful, it is crucial to attract and recruit the right affiliates who can effectively promote your brand. In this subchapter, we will delve into the insider secrets of attracting and recruiting affiliates, helping you crack the affiliate marketing code for marketing success.

First and foremost, it is essential to clearly define your target audience and niches within affiliate marketing. Understanding your target audience will enable you to identify potential affiliates who have a strong following within your niche. By focusing on affiliates who already have an established presence in your industry, you can leverage their credibility and reach to promote your products or services effectively.

To attract affiliates, it is crucial to offer an attractive commission structure. Affiliates are motivated by financial incentives, so ensure that your commission rates are competitive within the market. Additionally, consider offering performance-based bonuses and rewards to incentivize top-performing affiliates. Providing a clear and transparent commission structure will entice potential affiliates to join your program.

Another effective strategy is to provide affiliates with comprehensive marketing materials. Affiliates are more likely to promote your brand if they have access to high-quality banners, ads, product images, and compelling content. By equipping affiliates with the necessary tool and resources, you empower them to create engaging content that drives conversions.

Building strong relationships with your affiliates is crucial for long term success. Regularly communicate with your affiliates, provide them with updates on new products or upcoming promotions, and offer personalized support. By nurturing these relationships, you can foster loyalty and encourage affiliates to actively promote your brand.

Lastly, make it easy for potential affiliates to sign up and join you program. Streamline the application process, offer a user-friendly affiliate dashboard, and ensure prompt payment processing. The easier it is for affiliates to join and navigate your program, the more likely they are to choose your brand over competitors.

In conclusion, attracting and recruiting affiliates is a critical aspect o cracking the affiliate marketing code. By understanding your target audience, offering competitive commissions, providing comprehensive marketing materials, building strong relationships, and simplifying the onboarding process, you can attract top-notch affiliates who will drive your marketing success.

Developing Relationships with Affiliates

In the world of affiliate marketing, building strong and trustworthy relationships with affiliates is crucial for long-term success. As an affiliate marketer, you rely on the support and collaboration of affiliates to promote and sell your products or services. By nurturing these relationships, you can unlock a multitude of opportunities and take your marketing efforts to new heights.

The first step in developing relationships with affiliates is to understand their needs and motivations. Affiliates are driven by various factors, such as financial gain, product relevance, and credibility. Take the time to research and identify potential affiliates who align with your niche and target audience. Look for partners who have a genuine interest in your products or services and possess the skills and resources to effectively promote them.

Once you have identified potential affiliates, it is essential to establish open lines of communication. Reach out to them personally, introducing yourself and your brand. Show genuine interest in their work and understand how your products or services can add value to their audience. Be transparent about your affiliate program, including commission rates, promotional materials, and any unique selling points. By being upfront and clear, you can build trust and credibility from the beginning.

As you begin working with affiliates, provide them with the necessary tools and resources to succeed. This could include banner ads, product images, email templates, and exclusive promotions. These materials should be easily accessible and tailored to their specific needs. Additionally, consider offering incentives or bonuses for top-performing affiliates to encourage their continued dedication and loyalty.

Regularly monitor and analyze the performance of your affiliates. Use tracking software to keep track of their sales and conversions. This data will help you identify top-performing affiliates and optimize your marketing strategies accordingly. Recognize and reward their effort by offering increased commissions or exclusive collaborations. By acknowledging their hard work, you can foster a positive and mutually beneficial relationship.

Finally, never underestimate the power of ongoing support and communication. Stay connected with your affiliates through newsletters, webinars, or private forums. Provide them with industry insights, marketing tips, and exclusive updates to help them stay ahead of the curve. By nurturing these relationships and offering ongoing support, you can create a network of dedicated affiliates who are invested in your success.

In conclusion, developing relationships with affiliates is a fundamental aspect of affiliate marketing success. By understanding their needs, establishing open communication, providing necessary resources, monitoring performance, and offering ongoing support, you can build strong and mutually beneficial relationships with your affiliates. These partnerships will not only enhance your marketing efforts but also unlock new opportunities for growth and success in the ever-evolving world of affiliate marketing.

roviding Affiliate Support and Resources

n the fast-paced world of affiliate marketing, success lies not only in nding the right products to promote but also in having access to the ecessary support and resources. As a marketer in the affiliate narketing niche, it is crucial to understand the importance of roviding affiliate support and resources to your partners. This ubchapter will delve into the key strategies and insights needed to ffectively empower your affiliates and drive marketing success.

One of the most valuable resources you can provide to your affiliates is omprehensive training. By offering educational materials, webinars, nd workshops, you can equip your partners with the knowledge and kills they need to excel in their marketing efforts. Sharing insider ecrets, tips, and strategies will not only boost their confidence but also oster a sense of community and collaboration within your affiliate network.

Additionally, offering personalized support is essential in ensuring our affiliates feel valued and motivated. Establishing open lines of communication allows them to seek guidance, ask questions, and receive timely assistance. This can be achieved through email, chat support, or even a dedicated forum where affiliates can connect and share experiences. By providing prompt responses and being readily available, you demonstrate your commitment to their success.

Another effective way to support your affiliates is by providing them with high-quality marketing materials. These may include banner ads, email templates, product images, and persuasive sales copy. By offering a range of professionally designed assets, you enable your affiliates to create compelling campaigns that resonate with their audiences. Regularly updating and refreshing these resources ensures that your affiliates always have access to the latest promotions materials.

In addition to training and support, offering incentives and rewards can motivate your affiliates to go the extra mile. Consider implementing a tiered commission structure, where top-performing affiliates earn higher commissions or exclusive bonuses. Recognizing their achievements through a leaderboard or affiliate spotlight can also foster healthy competition and drive exceptional results.

Lastly, staying up-to-date with industry trends and sharing relevant insights with your affiliates is crucial. By providing them with the latest market research, emerging niches, and innovative strategies, you position your affiliates as knowledgeable experts in their field. This not only enhances their credibility but also strengthens your overall network.

In conclusion, providing affiliate support and resources is paramount to the success of your marketing efforts in the affiliate marketing niche. By offering comprehensive training, personalized support, high-quality marketing materials, incentives, and industry insights, you empower your affiliates to excel in their promotional activities. Remember, when your affiliates succeed, so do you.

Chapter 4: Creating Successful Affiliate Marketing Campaigns

Crafting Compelling Affiliate Offers

In the fast-paced world of affiliate marketing, the success of your campaigns largely depends on the quality and appeal of your affiliate offers. The ability to craft compelling offers can make all the difference between a lackluster campaign and one that generates substantial revenue. This subchapter will delve into the secrets of creating irresistible affiliate offers that will captivate your audience and drive conversions.

The first step in crafting compelling affiliate offers is understanding your target audience. Conduct thorough market research to identify their needs, pain points, and desires. This knowledge will equip you with valuable insights into the type of products or services that will resonate with them the most.

Next, leverage the power of storytelling to connect with your audience emotionally. Craft a compelling narrative around the affiliate offer, highlighting the unique features, benefits, and value it provides. Use relatable examples and testimonials to demonstrate how the offer has positively impacted others. By tapping into the emotions of your audience, you can create a sense of urgency and desire that drives them to take action.

Another crucial aspect of crafting compelling affiliate offers is ensuring that they align with the interests and preferences of your target audience. Tailor your offers to specific niches within the affiliate marketing industry to maximize their appeal. For example, if your audience consists of fitness enthusiasts, focus on promoting health and wellness products or workout programs that cater to their needs.

Moreover, providing added value to your audience can significantly enhance the appeal of your affiliate offers. Offer exclusive bonuses, discounts, or freebies that complement the main product or service. This not only incentivizes your audience to make a purchase but also differentiates your offer from competitors'. Additionally, consider creating informative and engaging content, such as ebooks, videos, or webinars, that educates your audience and establishes you as an authority in your niche.

Lastly, optimize your affiliate offers for different marketing channels. Tailor your messaging and creatives to suit various platforms, such as social media, email marketing, or paid advertising. This ensures that your offers effectively reach your target audience, increasing the likelihood of conversions.

Crafting compelling affiliate offers is an art that requires a deep understanding of your audience, effective storytelling, alignment with niche interests, providing added value, and optimizing for different marketing channels. By mastering these techniques, you can unlock the full potential of your affiliate marketing campaigns and achieve marketing success.

Designing Effective Landing Pages

In the fast-paced world of digital marketing, landing pages play a crucial role in driving conversions and boosting revenue. Whether you're a seasoned marketer or just starting your journey in affiliate marketing, understanding how to design effective landing pages is essential for success. This subchapter will provide you with insider secrets and valuable tips to create landing pages that captivate your audience and drive them towards taking the desired action.

The first step in designing an effective landing page is to clearly define your goal. Are you looking to generate leads, sell a product, or promote a specific offer? Once you have a clear objective in mind, you can tailor your landing page to meet that goal. Remember, simplicity is key. Keep your landing page focused on one call-to-action, ensuring that visitors are not distracted by unnecessary clutter.

Next, you need to create a compelling headline that grabs the attention of your target audience. A catchy headline that clearly communicates the value proposition of your offer will entice visitors to stay on your landing page and explore further. Make it clear what problem your product or service solves and why it is the best solution available.

Another crucial aspect of designing effective landing pages is the layout and design. A clean and visually appealing design with a clear hierarchy of information will guide visitors towards the desired action. Use eye-catching visuals, such as high-quality images or videos, to engage your audience and reinforce your message. Remember to keep your landing page mobile-friendly, as an increasing number of users access the internet through their smartphones.

Incorporating social proof into your landing page can significantl boost its effectiveness. Testimonials, customer reviews, and trus badges can help build trust and credibility, increasing the likelihood o conversion. Additionally, creating a sense of urgency through limited time offers or countdown timers can create a fear of missing out compelling visitors to take immediate action.

Lastly, always track and analyze the performance of your landing pages. A/B testing different elements, such as headlines, colors, or call to-action buttons, can provide valuable insights into what resonate best with your audience. Continuously optimizing your landing page. based on data-driven decisions will ensure that you maximize thei effectiveness and drive superior results.

Designing effective landing pages is an art that combines creativity psychology, and data analysis. By following the insider secrets and tip outlined in this subchapter, you will be well-equipped to create landing pages that not only captivate your audience but also drive conversions and propel your affiliate marketing success.

Implementing Conversion Optimization Techniques

In the competitive world of affiliate marketing, getting traffic to your website is just the first step towards success. The ultimate goal is to convert that traffic into paying customers. This is where conversion optimization techniques come into play. By implementing these strategies, you can maximize your chances of turning visitors into buyers and boosting your affiliate marketing revenue.

One crucial aspect of conversion optimization is understanding your target audience. Research and analyze the demographics, interests, and behavior of your target market. This information will help you tailor your website content and calls-to-action to appeal to their specific needs and desires. By understanding their pain points and offering solutions, you can increase the likelihood of conversions.

Another effective technique is optimizing your website's user experience (UX). A cluttered and confusing website can drive potential customers away. Ensure that your site is visually appealing, easy to navigate, and loads quickly. Implement clear and concise calls-to-action that guide visitors towards making a purchase. Test different layouts, color schemes, and button placements to determine what works best for your audience.

Furthermore, incorporating persuasive copywriting techniques can significantly impact conversion rates. Craft compelling headlines and product descriptions that grab attention and highlight the benefits of your affiliate products. Use storytelling to engage your audience emotionally and create a connection with them. Incorporate social proof, such as testimonials and reviews, to build trust and credibility.

Additionally, optimizing your website for mobile devices is crucial in today's digital landscape. With more people accessing the internet through smartphones and tablets, a mobile-friendly website is essential for capturing and converting mobile traffic. Ensure that your site is responsive, loads quickly on mobile devices, and offers a seamless browsing experience.

Moreover, leveraging data and analytics is essential for conversion optimization. Track and analyze key metrics such as bounce rate, time on site, and conversion rates. Identify areas of improvement and implement A/B testing to experiment with different variations of your website elements. Continuously monitor and refine your strategies based on data-driven insights.

In conclusion, implementing effective conversion optimization techniques is vital for success in affiliate marketing. By understanding your target audience, optimizing user experience, incorporating persuasive copywriting, optimizing for mobile, and leveraging data, you can maximize your conversions and increase your affiliate marketing revenue. Stay proactive and continually test and refine your strategies to stay ahead of the competition.

Utilizing Persuasive Copywriting Strategies

In the competitive world of affiliate marketing, persuasive copywriting can make all the difference between success and failure. The ability to craft compelling content that grabs the attention of your target audience and convinces them to take action is a skill that every marketer should strive to master. In this subchapter, we will delve into the world of persuasive copywriting strategies and explore how you can leverage them to achieve marketing success in the realm of affiliate marketing.

One of the most important aspects of persuasive copywriting is understanding your audience. As an affiliate marketer, it is crucial to identify the needs, desires, and pain points of your target market. By knowing your audience inside out, you can tailor your copy to resonate with them on a deep level. Whether it's addressing their problems or offering a solution to their pain points, persuasive copywriting ensures that your message is compelling and relevant.

Another key tactic in persuasive copywriting is to create a sense of urgency. By highlighting time-sensitive offers, limited availability, or exclusive deals, you can encourage your audience to take immediate action. People are more likely to make a purchase or sign up for a service if they feel that they might miss out on a valuable opportunity. By utilizing scarcity and urgency in your copy, you can motivate your audience to act quickly and increase your conversions.

Furthermore, using social proof can significantly enhance the persuasive power of your copy. Testimonials, case studies, and reviews from satisfied customers can instill trust and credibility in your audience. By showcasing the positive experiences of others, you can overcome any skepticism and persuade your audience to believe in your product or service. When your audience sees that others have benefited from what you are offering, they are more likely to follow suit.

Lastly, incorporating strong and compelling calls-to-action (CTAs) is essential in persuasive copywriting. A well-crafted CTA guides your audience towards taking the desired action, such as making a purchase, subscribing to a newsletter, or clicking on an affiliate link. By using action-oriented language and creating a sense of urgency, you can prompt your audience to act immediately, increasing the chances of conversions and affiliate commissions.

In conclusion, persuasive copywriting is a vital skill that every affiliate marketer should master. By understanding your audience, creating a sense of urgency, utilizing social proof, and incorporating compelling CTAs, you can significantly enhance your marketing success in the world of affiliate marketing. Cracking the code to persuasive copywriting is the key to unlocking the full potential of your affiliate marketing endeavors.

Chapter 5: Maximizing Affiliate Marketing Revenue

Implementing Effective Traffic Generation Methods

In the fast-paced world of affiliate marketing, driving consistent and high-quality traffic to your website is crucial for success. Without a steady stream of visitors, your affiliate marketing efforts can go to waste. This subchapter on "Implementing Effective Traffic Generation Methods" will provide you with insider secrets and strategies to boost your website's traffic and maximize your marketing success.

1. Search Engine Optimization (SEO): Start by optimizing your website for search engines. Research relevant keywords and incorporate them strategically into your website's content, meta tags, and URLs. Focus on creating valuable and informative content that aligns with your niche. By ranking higher in search engine results, you will attract organic traffic and increase your chances of acquiring potential customers.

2. Content Marketing: Develop a consistent content marketing strategy to engage and attract your target audience. Create valuable blog posts, articles, videos, and infographics that resonate with your niche. Share your content across various platforms, such as social media, forums, and industry-specific websites. This will establish your credibility and drive traffic back to your website.

3. Social Media Marketing: Leverage the power of social media platforms to reach a wider audience. Identify which platforms your target audience frequents and create engaging and shareable content. Build a strong presence by actively participating in conversations, engaging with your followers, and promoting your affiliate offers. Use

social media advertising to target specific demographics and increas your website's visibility.

4. Influencer Marketing: Collaborate with influential figures in you niche to increase your brand's visibility and attract their followers Identify key influencers who align with your products or services and negotiate partnerships or sponsored posts. By leveraging thei credibility and reach, you can tap into their loyal audience and drive traffic to your website.

5. Pay-Per-Click (PPC) Advertising: Consider investing in PPC advertising to drive immediate traffic to your website. Platforms like Google Ads and social media advertising allow you to target specific keywords, demographics, and interests, ensuring your ads reach the right audience. Monitor and optimize your campaigns regularly to maximize your ROI.

6. Email Marketing: Build an email list by offering valuable content or incentives to your website visitors. Develop an email marketing strategy to nurture your subscribers and drive traffic back to your website through newsletters, promotions, and personalized offers Segment your email list based on demographics and interests to deliver targeted content.

By implementing these effective traffic generation methods, you can significantly boost your website's visibility, attract a larger audience, and increase your chances of converting visitors into loyal customers. Remember, consistency and continuous optimization are key to long-term marketing success. Stay up-to-date with the latest trends and adapt your strategies accordingly to stay ahead in the competitive world of affiliate marketing.

everaging Social Media for Affiliate Marketing Success

n today's digital age, social media has become an indispensable tool or marketers, and affiliate marketers are no exception. With its vast each and ability to connect with a highly targeted audience, everaging social media platforms can significantly boost your affiliate narketing success. In this subchapter, we will explore how you can arness the power of social media to maximize your affiliate marketing fforts and drive substantial results.

'irst and foremost, understanding your target audience is crucial. By dentifying the specific demographics, interests, and preferences of our niche market, you can tailor your social media content to esonate with your audience effectively. Use platforms like Facebook, 'witter, Instagram, and LinkedIn to engage with your target market, hare valuable content, and build a loyal following.

)ne of the key benefits of social media is its ability to facilitate elationship-building. Building trust and credibility with your udience is essential in affiliate marketing. By regularly interacting vith your followers, responding to their comments, and addressing heir concerns, you can establish yourself as an authority in your niche. This will not only increase your brand's visibility but also enhance the likelihood of your audience engaging with your affiliate inks.

Another effective strategy is to create compelling and shareable content. Social media platforms thrive on engaging and viral content. Create visually appealing graphics, videos, and blog posts that provide value to your audience and encourage them to share with others. By creating content that educates, entertains, or solves a problem, you can position yourself as a reliable source of information, thereby increasing your chances of affiliate conversions.

Utilizing social media advertising is another powerful tool in your arsenal. Platforms like Facebook Ads, Instagram Ads, and Twitter Ads allow you to target specific demographics and interests, ensuring that your affiliate promotions reach the right audience. Craft compelling ad copy and use eye-catching visuals to capture attention and entice users to click on your affiliate links.

Lastly, tracking your social media efforts is essential for optimizing your affiliate marketing success. Make use of analytics tools provided by social media platforms to monitor the performance of your posts, ads, and affiliate links. This data will help you identify what strategies are working and what needs improvement, enabling you to refine your approach and maximize your return on investment.

In conclusion, leveraging social media for affiliate marketing success is a game-changer for marketers in the affiliate marketing niche. By understanding your target audience, building relationships, creating shareable content, utilizing social media advertising, and tracking your efforts, you can harness the immense potential of social media to drive significant results in your affiliate marketing endeavors. Embrace social media as a powerful asset and unlock the doors to marketing success in the affiliate space.

Harnessing the Power of Email Marketing

Email marketing has emerged as a game-changing tool in the world of affiliate marketing. With a wide reach and an ability to personalize messages, it has become an integral part of successful marketing campaigns. In this subchapter, we will explore how to harness the power of email marketing to maximize your affiliate marketing efforts.

First and foremost, building a strong email list is crucial. A quality email list allows you to target potential customers who have already shown interest in your niche or product. To build your list, offer valuable incentives such as free e-books, exclusive discounts, or access to premium content. Make sure to place opt-in forms strategically on your website and landing pages to capture email addresses effectively.

Once you have a substantial email list, segmentation becomes essential. Dividing your subscribers into different segments based on their interests, demographics, or buying behavior allows you to send more personalized and relevant emails. Tailoring your messages to specific segments increases engagement, click-through rates, and ultimately, conversions.

Crafting compelling email content is equally important. Your emails should be concise, engaging, and visually appealing. Use attention-grabbing subject lines and include a clear call-to-action that entices readers to take the desired action. Experiment with different email formats, such as newsletters, product updates, or promotional offers, to keep your subscribers interested and engaged.

Automation is a powerful tool in email marketing. Set up automated email sequences to nurture your leads and guide them through the sales funnel. Welcome emails, abandoned cart reminders, and post-purchase follow-ups are just a few examples of automated emails that can significantly impact your conversion rates. By leveraging automation, you can deliver timely and relevant content without manually sending each email.

It is also crucial to track and analyze the performance of your email campaigns. Pay attention to metrics like open rates, click-through rates, and conversions to gain insights into what works and what doesn't. A/B testing different elements of your emails, such as subject lines, visuals, or call-to-action buttons, can help optimize your campaigns for better results.

In summary, email marketing is a powerful tool in the affiliate marketing arsenal. By building a quality email list, segmenting your subscribers, crafting compelling content, implementing automation, and analyzing performance, you can harness the power of email marketing to drive conversions and achieve marketing success in the competitive world of affiliate marketing.

Exploring Advanced Affiliate Marketing Techniques

Welcome to the subchapter on "Exploring Advanced Affiliate Marketing Techniques" from the book "Cracking the Affiliate Code: Insider Secrets for Marketing Success." In this section, we will delve deeper into the world of affiliate marketing, focusing on advanced strategies and techniques that can take your affiliate marketing efforts to the next level.

Affiliate marketing is a dynamic and ever-evolving field, and staying ahead of the game requires continuous learning and innovation. This subchapter is specifically designed for marketers who are already familiar with the basics of affiliate marketing and are looking to expand their knowledge base to drive even greater success in the niche of affiliate marketing.

In this subchapter, we will explore various advanced techniques that successful affiliate marketers employ to maximize their earning potential. We will discuss topics such as:

1. Advanced Tracking and Analytics: Learn how to utilize advanced tracking tools and analytics platforms to gain deeper insights into your affiliate campaigns. Discover how to measure key performance indicators (KPIs) effectively and optimize your campaigns based on data-driven insights.

2. Advanced SEO Strategies: Explore advanced search engine optimization (SEO) techniques specific to affiliate marketing. Discover how to optimize your website and content for better organic rankings, drive targeted traffic, and increase your affiliate conversions.

3. Influencer Marketing: Uncover the power of influencer marketing and learn how to collaborate with influencers to promote your affiliate

products effectively. Discover strategies to identify, approach, and build mutually beneficial relationships with influencers in your niche.

4. Email Marketing Automation: Harness the power of email marketing automation to build a loyal subscriber base, nurture relationships, and promote affiliate products effectively. Learn advanced techniques such as segmentation, personalization, and automated funnels to maximize your email marketing efforts.

5. Advanced Social Media Strategies: Explore advanced social media marketing techniques and platforms that can help you reach a wider audience and drive more affiliate sales. Discover how to leverage social media ad campaigns, create engaging content, and build a thriving community around your affiliate products.

By exploring these advanced affiliate marketing techniques, you will gain a competitive edge in the affiliate marketing niche. Whether you are an experienced affiliate marketer or just starting your journey, this subchapter will provide you with valuable insights and strategies to take your affiliate marketing efforts to new heights.

Remember, affiliate marketing is not a get-rich-quick scheme but rather a long-term, sustainable business model. By incorporating these advanced techniques into your marketing arsenal, you will be better equipped to create profitable affiliate campaigns and achieve marketing success.

Chapter 6: Analytics and Tracking for Affiliate Marketing

Understanding Key Performance Indicators (KPIs)

In the realm of affiliate marketing, understanding and effectively utilizing key performance indicators (KPIs) is crucial for achieving marketing success. KPIs provide marketers with measurable data that can help evaluate the performance and effectiveness of their affiliate campaigns. By tracking and analyzing these metrics, marketers can gain valuable insights into their strategies, make data-driven decisions, and optimize their campaigns for maximum profitability.

One of the most important KPIs in affiliate marketing is conversion rate. Conversion rate measures the percentage of website visitors who take the desired action, such as making a purchase or filling out a form. It is a direct indicator of campaign effectiveness and can help marketers identify areas for improvement. By analyzing conversion rates and comparing them across different campaigns or traffic sources, marketers can identify the most successful strategies and allocate resources accordingly.

Another crucial KPI in affiliate marketing is return on investment (ROI). ROI measures the profitability of a campaign by comparing the revenue generated to the cost of running the campaign. It helps marketers determine whether their efforts are generating enough revenue to justify the expenses incurred. By tracking ROI, marketers can identify underperforming campaigns and either optimize or discontinue them, thus maximizing their overall profitability.

Click-through rate (CTR) is another important KPI in affiliate marketing. It measures the percentage of users who click on an affiliate link or advertisement. A high CTR indicates that the marketing message is compelling and the targeting is effective. By monitoring CTR and experimenting with different ad formats or messaging, marketers can improve their campaigns and drive more traffic to their affiliate offers.

Additionally, tracking customer acquisition cost (CAC) is essential for affiliate marketers. CAC measures the cost of acquiring a new customer and helps marketers evaluate the effectiveness of their acquisition strategies. By comparing CAC to the lifetime value of a customer, marketers can determine whether their campaigns are generating profitable results.

Overall, understanding and utilizing key performance indicators is essential for success in affiliate marketing. By tracking and analyzing metrics such as conversion rate, ROI, CTR, and CAC, marketers can make data-driven decisions and optimize their campaigns for maximum profitability. It is important to regularly evaluate these KPIs, experiment with different strategies, and continuously improve marketing efforts to achieve long-term success in the competitive world of affiliate marketing.

Tracking Affiliate Performance and Conversions

In the fast-paced world of affiliate marketing, tracking performance and conversions is crucial to achieving marketing success. Without the ability to measure and analyze the effectiveness of your affiliate campaigns, it becomes challenging to optimize your strategies and maximize your returns. This subchapter will guide you through the essential aspects of tracking affiliate performance and conversions, empowering you to make data-driven decisions that will drive your marketing efforts forward.

1. Setting up a Tracking System: To effectively track your affiliate performance and conversions, you need to implement a robust tracking system. This system should allow you to monitor various key performance indicators (KPIs), such as click-through rates (CTR), conversion rates, and average order values. By integrating tracking pixels and unique affiliate links, you can capture valuable data about your audience's behavior and their interactions with your affiliate campaigns.

2. Choosing the Right Metrics: Understanding which metrics to track is vital to evaluating your affiliate marketing efforts accurately. While metrics like the number of clicks and impressions provide some insight, it is crucial to focus on key metrics that align with your campaign goals and desired outcomes. These might include conversion rates, revenue per click (RPC), customer lifetime value (CLV), and return on investment (ROI).

3. Utilizing Analytics Tools: Leveraging analytics tools can significantly simplify the tracking process and provide you with in-depth insights into your affiliate performance. Popular tools like Google Analytics and affiliate network

reporting platforms offer comprehensive tracking capabilities allowing you to measure campaign performance, identify top performing affiliates, and detect areas for improvement.

4. A/B Testing and Optimization To improve your affiliate marketing performance, it is essential to continually test and optimize your campaigns. A/B testing different creatives, landing pages, and call-to-action elements can provide valuable insights into what resonates best with your target audience. By analyzing the results and making data-driven optimizations, you can increase conversions and maximize your affiliate marketing success.

5. Performance-Based Incentives Implementing performance-based incentives can motivate your affiliates to drive better results. By offering tiered commission structures or bonuses for achieving specific performance milestones, you can encourage your affiliates to put in the extra effort and enhance their performance. Additionally, providing them with real-time access to performance data can enable them to optimize their efforts and increase their conversions.

Tracking affiliate performance and conversions is an integral part of cracking the affiliate code and achieving marketing success. By implementing a robust tracking system, focusing on the right metrics, utilizing analytics tools, conducting A/B testing, and implementing performance-based incentives, you can optimize your affiliate marketing campaigns and drive significant results. Remember, data is power in the world of affiliate marketing, and leveraging it effectively will give you a competitive edge in the ever-evolving digital landscape.

Analyzing Data to Optimize Campaigns

In the ever-evolving world of affiliate marketing, success lies in the ability to constantly adapt and optimize your campaigns. One of the most effective ways to achieve this is by analyzing data. Data analysis allows marketers to gain valuable insights into the performance of their campaigns, enabling them to make informed decisions and maximize their marketing success.

When it comes to analyzing data, it is essential to track and measure key performance indicators (KPIs) that are relevant to your affiliate marketing campaigns. These KPIs can vary depending on your niche, but some common ones include click-through rates (CTR), conversion rates, average order value (AOV), and return on ad spend (ROAS). By monitoring these metrics, you can identify which aspects of your campaign are performing well and which need improvement.

There are various tools and techniques available to help you gather and analyze the data effectively. Tracking software, such as Google Analytics or affiliate network tracking platforms, can provide you with valuable data on user behavior, traffic sources, and conversion rates. It is important to set up proper tracking mechanisms to ensure accurate and reliable data collection.

Once you have collected the data, it's time to dive into the analysis process. Start by identifying patterns and trends in the data. Are there specific days or times when your campaigns perform better? Are there certain demographics or locations that generate higher conversions? By answering these questions, you can optimize your campaigns to target the most profitable audience segments.

Data analysis can also help you uncover potential issues or bottleneck in your campaigns. For example, if you notice a high bounce rate on particular landing page, you can investigate the reasons behind it an make necessary improvements. Similarly, if a specific ad creative i underperforming, you can experiment with different variations to se what resonates best with your target audience.

Furthermore, data analysis can reveal valuable insights about you competitors' strategies. By benchmarking your performance agains industry averages and studying your competitors' campaigns, you car identify areas where you can outperform them and gain a competitive edge.

In conclusion, analyzing data is a crucial step in optimizing you affiliate marketing campaigns. By tracking and measuring relevan KPIs, using appropriate tools, and interpreting the data effectively, you can make data-driven decisions to improve your campaigns performance. Remember, the key to success lies in constant adaptation and optimization, and data analysis is your secret weapon in cracking the affiliate marketing code.

Chapter 7: Compliance and Legal Considerations in Affiliate Marketing

Adhering to FTC Guidelines

In the world of affiliate marketing, it is essential to understand and adhere to the guidelines set forth by the Federal Trade Commission (FTC). These guidelines are designed to protect consumers and ensure transparency in marketing practices. By following these guidelines, marketers can build trust with their audience and maintain a positive reputation in the industry.

One of the key aspects of FTC guidelines is the requirement for full disclosure. When promoting products or services as an affiliate, it is crucial to disclose any financial relationships or incentives that may influence the content being shared. This means clearly stating when you are receiving compensation for promoting a product or service. Whether it is through affiliate links, sponsorships, or any other form of compensation, transparency is key. Failure to disclose these relationships can lead to legal consequences and damage to your reputation.

Another important guideline to follow is the prohibition of deceptive practices. The FTC prohibits false or misleading advertising, including making unsubstantiated claims about a product or service. It is vital to ensure that any claims made in marketing materials are supported by evidence or honest experiences. Misleading consumers can result in legal action and harm your credibility as an affiliate marketer.

Additionally, the FTC requires marketers to avoid unfair competition practices. This means refraining from engaging in any activities that may unfairly disadvantage competitors or mislead consumers. This includes tactics such as false endorsements, fake reviews, or manipulating search engine rankings. Operating with integrity and providing genuine value to your audience is essential to long-term success in affiliate marketing.

To ensure compliance with FTC guidelines, marketers should be proactive in staying informed about any updates or changes to the regulations. The FTC provides resources and guidelines on their website that can help marketers understand and comply with the rules. It is also advisable to consult with legal professionals or industry experts who specialize in affiliate marketing to ensure you are following best practices.

By adhering to FTC guidelines, marketers can build trust with their audience, maintain a positive reputation, and avoid legal repercussions. Transparency, honesty, and integrity are the pillars of successful affiliate marketing. By prioritizing these principles, marketers can create long-lasting relationships with their audience and achieve marketing success.

Understanding Affiliate Disclosure Requirements

One of the essential aspects of successful affiliate marketing is maintaining transparency and building trust with your audience. To achieve this, it is crucial to understand and comply with the affiliate disclosure requirements. In this subchapter, we will delve into the importance of disclosing affiliate relationships, explore the legal obligations, and provide practical tips on how to effectively incorporate disclosures into your marketing strategies.

Affiliate marketing is a powerful tool that allows marketers to earn commissions by promoting products or services. However, it is vital to disclose any financial relationships you have with the brands you promote. Why? Because transparency builds trust. When your audience knows that you may receive compensation for the products you recommend, they can make informed decisions and feel confident that your recommendations are unbiased.

From a legal standpoint, the Federal Trade Commission (FTC) in the United States and similar regulatory bodies worldwide require affiliate marketers to disclose their relationships with the brands they promote. Failure to comply with these guidelines can result in hefty fines and damage to your reputation. Therefore, understanding the rules and implementing proper disclosures is not just an ethical obligation but also a legal one.

So, how do you effectively disclose your affiliate relationships? The key is to make the disclosure clear, conspicuous, and easily understandable to your audience. It should be placed where it is impossible to miss, such as at the beginning of your content or right next to affiliate links. A simple statement like "This post contains affiliate links. If you make a purchase through these links, I may earn commission" is usually sufficient.

In addition to written disclosures, visual cues like badges or banner can also be effective. However, it is important to avoid misleading o deceptive practices that may downplay or hide the disclosure Remember, the ultimate goal is to be transparent and ensure that you audience can easily recognize your affiliate relationships.

To incorporate disclosures seamlessly into your marketing strategies consider integrating them into your content naturally. For example you can share personal experiences, provide honest reviews, anc explain why you genuinely believe in the products or services you are promoting. By doing so, you not only meet the disclosure requirements but also strengthen your credibility and build a loya following.

In conclusion, understanding affiliate disclosure requirements is essential for every marketer involved in affiliate marketing. By complying with these obligations, you create a transparent and trustworthy relationship with your audience, which ultimately contributes to your long-term success. Remember to always stay updated on the latest guidelines and make disclosing your affiliate relationships a priority in your marketing efforts.

Navigating International Affiliate Marketing Laws

In today's interconnected world, affiliate marketing has become a global phenomenon. As marketers, it is crucial to understand the international laws and regulations that govern this dynamic industry. This subchapter will delve into the intricacies of navigating international affiliate marketing laws, equipping you with the knowledge to succeed in this ever-expanding marketplace.

One of the primary challenges in affiliate marketing is complying with the diverse legal frameworks across different countries. Each jurisdiction has its own set of rules and regulations, ranging from consumer protection laws to privacy and data protection regulations. Understanding these laws is essential to ensure your marketing campaigns are both effective and legally compliant.

When expanding your affiliate marketing efforts internationally, it is crucial to conduct thorough research on the laws and regulations of each target country. This includes understanding the legal requirements for advertising, disclosures, and data collection practices. Failure to comply with these laws can result in hefty fines, legal disputes, and reputational damage.

Consumer protection laws vary significantly across borders. It is important to understand the requirements for clear and transparent advertising, including accurate product descriptions and pricing information. Additionally, some countries have specific regulations governing affiliate marketing, such as requiring clear disclosure of the affiliate relationship between the marketer and the product or service being promoted.

Privacy and data protection regulations are another critical aspect of international affiliate marketing. As marketers, you must be aware of the data collection practices allowed in each jurisdiction and ensure compliance with local data protection laws. This may involve obtaining explicit consent from users before collecting their personal information and ensuring secure storage and processing of data.

Intellectual property laws also play a significant role in international affiliate marketing. Trademark infringement and copyright violation can have severe consequences, including legal action and financial penalties. It is important to understand the intellectual property right of the products or services being promoted and ensure compliance with applicable laws.

In conclusion, navigating international affiliate marketing law requires a comprehensive understanding of the legal landscape in each target country. By conducting thorough research, adhering to consumer protection laws, complying with privacy and data protection regulations, and respecting intellectual property rights marketers can ensure successful and legally compliant affiliate marketing campaigns. Familiarizing yourself with these international laws will not only protect your business but also enhance your reputation as a trustworthy and responsible marketer in the global affiliate marketing niche.

Chapter 8: Scaling and Growing Your Affiliate Business

Strategies for Scaling Affiliate Campaigns

In the fast-paced world of affiliate marketing, scaling your campaigns is essential to stay ahead of the competition and maximize your profits. To truly crack the affiliate code and achieve marketing success, you need to implement effective strategies that allow you to scale your affiliate campaigns efficiently. Here are some insider secrets to help you achieve just that.

1. Build a Solid Foundation: Before scaling your affiliate campaigns, it's crucial to have a solid foundation in place. This means conducting thorough research to identify profitable niches, understanding your target audience, and selecting the right affiliate programs that align with your niche and audience's interests. By starting with a strong foundation, you'll be better equipped to handle the challenges that come with scaling.

2. Optimize Your Landing Pages: A well-optimized landing page is the key to converting your traffic into paying customers. To scale your campaigns effectively, it's important to continually test and optimize your landing pages. Experiment with different headlines, call-to-actions, and layouts to find the winning combination that maximizes conversions. Remember, even small improvements can have a significant impact on your overall campaign performance.

3. Leverage Data and Analytics: Scaling affiliate campaigns requires a data-driven approach. Analyze your campaign data to identify patterns, trends, and areas of improvement. Use tracking tools and

analytics platforms to gain insights into your audience's behavior, conversion rates, and ROI. This information will help you make informed decisions when scaling your campaigns, allowing you to allocate your resources effectively.

4. Automate and Delegate: As your campaigns grow, managing everything manually becomes impractical. To scale efficiently, consider automating repetitive tasks and delegating responsibilities to a team or virtual assistants. Use tools and software that can streamline processes such as keyword research, ad creation, and campaign tracking. By automating and delegating, you'll free up time to focus on strategic planning and optimization.

5. Expand Your Traffic Sources: Scaling your affiliate campaigns often necessitates diversifying your traffic sources. Relying solely on one traffic channel can be risky, as changes in algorithms or policies can have a significant impact on your campaign's performance. Explore different traffic sources such as search engine optimization, social media advertising, influencer partnerships, and email marketing. By diversifying your traffic sources, you'll reach a wider audience and reduce dependency on a single channel.

6. Collaborate and Network: Networking and collaborating with other marketers in the affiliate marketing industry can provide valuable insights and opportunities for scaling your campaigns. Attend industry events, join online communities, and engage with other marketers to learn from their experiences and share best practices. Collaborating with influencers or affiliate networks can also help you tap into new markets and reach a broader audience.

Scaling affiliate campaigns requires a strategic and data-driven approach. By implementing these insider strategies, you'll be well on our way to cracking the affiliate code and achieving marketing success. Remember, scaling is an ongoing process, so constantly monitor and optimize your campaigns to stay ahead of the game.

Expanding Your Affiliate Network

In the world of affiliate marketing, building a strong network is crucial for long-term success. The more affiliates you have promoting your products or services, the greater your chances of reaching a wider audience and maximizing your revenue. This subchapter will provide you with valuable insights on how to effectively expand your affiliate network and take your affiliate marketing efforts to new heights.

1.   Establish   Clear   Goals
Before diving into expanding your affiliate network, it's essential to set clear goals. Define what you aim to achieve by expanding your network. Whether it's increasing sales, reaching a new target market, or boosting brand awareness, having a clear vision will help you make informed decisions and guide your efforts.

2.   Nurture   Relationships
Building strong relationships with your existing affiliates is just as important as acquiring new ones. Create a supportive and collaborative environment by offering personalized support, regular communication, and incentives to help them thrive. By fostering loyalty and trust, your affiliates will be more inclined to promote your products consistently and attract new affiliates to join your network.

3.   Leverage   Affiliate   Directories:
Affiliate directories are a goldmine for finding potential affiliates. These platforms connect affiliate marketers with businesses in various niches. Research and identify directories that cater to your target market and reach out to potential affiliates who align with your brand values and audience. Be prepared to offer them compelling incentives that make joining your network an attractive proposition.

. Attend Industry Events: Networking events, conferences, and trade shows are fantastic opportunities to connect with like-minded marketers and potential affiliates. By attending these events, you can not only expand your network but also gain valuable industry insights, stay updated on trends, and build relationships that can lead to fruitful collaborations. Be sure to approach these events with a clear pitch and presentation to attract potential affiliates.

. Create Quality Content: Content marketing is an effective strategy to attract high-quality affiliates. Produce valuable and engaging content that showcases your expertise and demonstrates the benefits of joining your network. Promote your content through various channels, such as your website, social media platforms, and industry forums, to increase visibility and attract potential affiliates who resonate with your message.

. Offer Competitive Commission Structures: Attractive commission structures are a powerful incentive for affiliates to join and promote your products or services. Research your competitors' commission rates and create a competitive structure that rewards your affiliates generously. Remember, a higher commission can attract more affiliates and motivate them to work harder to drive sales.

Expanding your affiliate network requires strategic planning, relationship-building, and offering enticing incentives. By implementing these strategies, you'll be well on your way to growing a thriving network of affiliates who will help you achieve your marketing goals and increase your revenue.

Diversifying Revenue Streams in Affiliate Marketing

In the fast-paced world of digital marketing, affiliate marketing has emerged as a powerful strategy for individuals and businesses looking to monetize their online presence. By promoting products and services of other companies, affiliates can earn a commission for every sale or lead generated through their marketing efforts. While this can be lucrative endeavor, relying solely on one affiliate program or a limited number of revenue streams is not a sustainable approach in the long run. To truly thrive in the competitive landscape of affiliate marketing, diversifying revenue streams is key.

One effective way to diversify revenue streams in affiliate marketing is by exploring different niches or verticals. By venturing beyond a single market, marketers can tap into new audiences and expand their reach. For instance, if you specialize in promoting beauty products, consider branching out into health and wellness or fashion. This diversification not only allows you to capture a wider customer base, but it also reduces the risk of fluctuations in a single niche.

Another approach to diversifying revenue streams is by partnering with multiple affiliate programs. Instead of relying solely on one program, explore different networks and platforms to find complementary products or services to promote. This way, you can create a diversified portfolio of affiliate partnerships, ensuring a steady flow of income even if one program experiences a downturn.

Additionally, consider incorporating other monetization methods alongside affiliate marketing. For instance, you can explore display advertising, sponsored content, or even creating and selling your own digital products or services. By diversifying your revenue streams, you an leverage your existing audience and expertise to generate dditional income beyond affiliate commissions.

urthermore, don't overlook the power of building your own brand. y establishing yourself as an authority within your niche, you can ttract direct sponsorships and collaborations with businesses, further iversifying your revenue streams. This can involve creating valuable ontent, engaging with your audience through social media, and ctively seeking partnerships with relevant brands.

n conclusion, diversifying revenue streams is crucial for long-term uccess in affiliate marketing. By exploring different niches, partnering vith multiple affiliate programs, incorporating other monetization nethods, and building your own brand, you can mitigate risks and naximize your earning potential. Remember, the key to cracking the ffiliate code lies in embracing diversity and adaptability in your narketing strategies.

Chapter 9: Overcoming Challenges in Affiliate Marketing

Dealing with Affiliate Fraud and Scams

In the dynamic world of affiliate marketing, where online businesse strive to maximize their reach and revenue through strategi partnerships, the unfortunate reality is that fraud and scams are persistent threat. As an affiliate marketer, it is crucial to be aware c these risks and take proactive measures to protect yourself and you business. This subchapter will guide you through the key aspects o dealing with affiliate fraud and scams, equipping you with th knowledge and tools to navigate this challenging landscape.

First and foremost, understanding the different types of affiliate frauc is essential. From cookie stuffing and ad stacking to fake leads anc unauthorized promotion, fraudsters employ various tactics to exploi the affiliate marketing ecosystem. By familiarizing yourself with thes fraudulent practices, you can identify warning signs and take swif action against any suspicious activity.

One effective way to combat affiliate fraud is by implementing robus monitoring and tracking systems. Investing in reliable trackin software allows you to track and analyze the performance of you affiliate campaigns, enabling you to detect any irregularities o discrepancies in real-time. Additionally, setting up stringent approva processes for new affiliates and closely scrutinizing their promotiona methods can help weed out potential fraudsters before they can cause harm.

Collaborating with reputable affiliate networks is another crucial step in safeguarding your business from scams. Reputable networks have stringent vetting procedures in place to ensure the legitimacy of their affiliates, reducing the risk of fraudulent activity. Furthermore, they often provide additional security measures, such as fraud detection tools and dedicated support teams, to mitigate the impact of scams on their affiliates.

In the event that you do encounter affiliate fraud, swift action is paramount. Promptly reporting any suspicious activity to your affiliate network or relevant authorities can help prevent further damage and hold the fraudsters accountable. Additionally, maintaining open lines of communication with your network and fellow affiliate marketers can facilitate the sharing of information and best practices, creating a united front against fraudsters.

Remember, staying vigilant and proactive is the key to mitigating the risks associated with affiliate fraud and scams. By continually educating yourself on the latest fraud trends, implementing robust tracking systems, collaborating with reputable networks, and taking swift action when necessary, you can protect your business and ensure long-term success in the competitive world of affiliate marketing.

Cracking the Affiliate Code: Insider Secrets for Marketing Success provides even more in-depth insights and strategies to help you navigate the affiliate marketing landscape successfully.

Managing Competition in the Affiliate Space

In the fast-paced world of affiliate marketing, competition i inevitable. As more and more marketers enter the affiliate space, i becomes crucial to adopt effective strategies to stay ahead of the game This subchapter aims to provide valuable insights and insider secret to manage competition in the affiliate space successfully.

1. Build a Solid Foundation: To effectively manage competition, it i essential to have a strong foundation. Start by selecting the right nich for your affiliate marketing efforts. Conduct thorough market researcl to identify the demand, competition, and potential profitability of you chosen niche. This will help you develop a unique selling propositior (USP) that sets you apart from your competitors.

2. Develop Strategic Partnerships: In affiliate marketing, forming strategic partnerships can be a game-changer. Collaborate with othe marketers, influencers, and industry experts to leverage their expertise and expand your reach. Establishing mutually beneficial relationships can open doors to new opportunities and help you stand out in a crowded market.

3. Focus on Quality Content: Content is king in the affiliate space Create high-quality, informative, and engaging content that resonates with your target audience. Providing valuable insights and actionable tips will not only attract visitors but also build trust and credibility. By consistently delivering exceptional content, you can differentiate yourself from competitors who may prioritize quantity over quality.

4. Optimize SEO and Keywords: Search engine optimization (SEO) plays a crucial role in managing competition. Conduct keyword research to identify relevant keywords and phrases that will drive

rganic traffic to your website or landing pages. By optimizing your ontent for search engines, you can increase your visibility and utrank your competitors in search results.

. Stay Updated with Industry Trends: The affiliate marketing indscape is constantly evolving. Stay ahead of the competition by taying informed about the latest industry trends, technological dvancements, and algorithm changes. By continuously learning and dapting your strategies, you can stay relevant and maintain a ompetitive edge.

. Monitor and Analyze Competitors: It is vital to keep a close eye on our competitors. Monitor their marketing strategies, promotions, and fferings to identify areas where you can improve or differentiate ourself. Use competitive analysis tools to gain insights into their erformance, keywords, and backlinks, enabling you to make data-riven decisions to outperform them.

n conclusion, managing competition in the affiliate space requires a ombination of strategic thinking, continuous learning, and daptation. By building a solid foundation, forming strategic artnerships, creating quality content, optimizing SEO, staying pdated with industry trends, and analyzing competitors, you can osition yourself as a leader in the affiliate marketing niche. Embrace ompetition as a driving force for innovation and growth, and strive to ffer unique value to your target audience.

Staying Updated with Industry Changes and Trends

In the ever-evolving world of marketing, it is crucial to stay update with industry changes and trends, especially in the niche of affiliat marketing. As an affiliate marketer, your success relies heavily on you ability to adapt to the latest advancements and strategies in the field This subchapter will equip you with the necessary tools and knowledg to stay ahead of the game and maximize your marketing success.

The first step in staying updated is to make a habit of regularly reading industry publications and blogs. Subscribe to reputable marketing magazines and websites that cover topics specific to affiliat marketing. This will ensure that you are always in the loop regarding the latest trends, techniques, and best practices. Stay informed abou emerging technologies, changes in algorithms, new platforms, and any other relevant updates that could impact your marketing efforts.

Another effective way to stay updated is by attending industry conferences and networking events. These gatherings provide a valuable opportunity to connect with fellow marketers, industry experts, and thought leaders. Engage in conversations, share experiences, and learn from others' successes and failures. The knowledge and insights gained from these events can be invaluable in shaping your marketing strategies and staying ahead of the competition.

Additionally, staying updated with industry changes requires a mindset of continuous learning. Invest time in online courses webinars, and workshops that focus on affiliate marketing. This will not only expand your knowledge but also provide you with the latest tips, tricks, and techniques that successful marketers are utilizing mbrace the ever-evolving nature of the industry and commit to ngoing education to ensure you stay on top of your game.

urthermore, staying updated with industry changes and trends also nvolves monitoring your competitors. Keep a close eye on their trategies, campaigns, and tactics. Analyze their successes and failures, nd identify areas where you can differentiate yourself. By nderstanding what works and what doesn't in your niche, you can nake informed decisions and optimize your own marketing efforts ccordingly.

n conclusion, staying updated with industry changes and trends is an ssential component of affiliate marketing success. By staying nformed through industry publications, attending conferences, ontinuous learning, and monitoring competitors, you can position ourself as a knowledgeable and adaptable marketer. Embrace the ver-evolving nature of the industry, and remember that staying ahead f the curve will ensure your continued growth and success in the vorld of affiliate marketing.

Chapter 10: The Future of Affiliate Marketing

The Evolution of Affiliate Marketing Technology

In the fast-paced world of marketing, staying ahead of the curve is crucial to success. One area that has seen significant evolution over the years is affiliate marketing, a niche that has become increasingl popular among marketers. In this subchapter, we will explore th fascinating journey of affiliate marketing technology and its impact o the industry.

Affiliate marketing, at its core, is a performance-based marketing model where affiliates are rewarded for driving traffic or sales to merchant's website. In the early days, this process was relativel manual, with affiliates relying on links and codes to track thei referrals. However, with the advent of technology, the landscap quickly transformed.

The first major evolution came with the introduction of affiliat networks. These networks acted as intermediaries between merchant and affiliates, providing a platform for tracking, reporting, and payment processing. This development allowed for a mor streamlined and efficient affiliate marketing process, connecting marketers with a wide range of products and services.

As technology advanced, so did the tools available to affiliate marketers. With the rise of e-commerce and the internet, tracking became more sophisticated, enabling affiliates to monitor thei performance in real-time. The introduction of cookies and tracking pixels further revolutionized the industry, providing marketers with valuable insights into consumer behavior and enabling more targeted marketing strategies.

The rise of social media platforms brought about another wave of change in affiliate marketing technology. With the ability to reach vast audiences and leverage influencers, marketers found new avenues for promoting products and driving sales. Social media tracking tools and analytics allowed for more precise targeting and measurement, empowering affiliates to optimize their campaigns for maximum results.

Today, affiliate marketing technology continues to evolve rapidly, driven by advancements in artificial intelligence and machine learning. These technologies enable marketers to automate processes, personalize offers, and predict consumer behavior. With the help of AI-powered algorithms, affiliates can optimize their campaigns at an unprecedented level, ensuring they reach the right audience at the right time.

In conclusion, the evolution of affiliate marketing technology has transformed the industry, making it more accessible, efficient, and profitable. From manual tracking to sophisticated analytics and AI-powered optimization, the journey of affiliate marketing technology is a testament to the power of innovation in marketing. As marketers in the affiliate marketing niche, it is crucial to stay abreast of these advancements and harness the full potential of technology to achieve marketing success.

Predictions and Trends for the Affiliate Marketing Industry

As the world of digital marketing continues to evolve, the affiliate marketing industry is also undergoing significant transformations. In this subchapter, we will explore the predictions and trends that are shaping the future of affiliate marketing, specifically addressing the needs and interests of the marketing audience and those involved in the affiliate marketing niche.

1. Rise of Influencer Marketing: With the growing influence of social media platforms, influencer marketing has become a powerful tool for brands to reach their target audience. In the affiliate marketing industry, we can expect to see a surge in collaborations between brands and influencers. Affiliate marketers will need to adapt by building strong relationships with influencers to leverage their reach and engagement.

2. Expansion of Niche Markets: As traditional markets become saturated, niche markets are gaining momentum. Affiliate marketers who can identify and target these niche markets will have a competitive edge. This requires a deep understanding of specific customer segments, allowing marketers to deliver tailored content and products that resonate with their unique needs and interests.

3. Mobile Optimization: With the increasing use of smartphones and tablets, optimizing affiliate marketing strategies for mobile devices is crucial. Mobile-friendly websites, responsive designs, and mobile-specific campaigns will become essential for success in the industry. Affiliate marketers must ensure that their content is easily accessible and visually appealing across various devices.

. Emphasis on Video Content: Video consumption is on the rise, and has become a powerful medium for engaging audiences. Affiliate marketers should invest in creating high-quality video content to capture the attention of their target audience. From product reviews to tutorials and testimonials, incorporating video content into affiliate marketing strategies will yield higher conversion rates and engagement.

. Artificial Intelligence and Automation: The implementation of artificial intelligence (AI) and automation tools is revolutionizing the affiliate marketing landscape. AI-powered algorithms can analyze vast amounts of data, enabling marketers to make data-driven decisions and optimize their campaigns for better results. Automation tools can streamline repetitive tasks, allowing marketers to focus on strategy and creativity.

. Enhanced Personalization: As customers seek more personalized experiences, affiliate marketers need to deliver targeted content that caters to individual preferences. By leveraging customer data and segmentation techniques, marketers can provide tailored recommendations and offers, resulting in higher conversions and customer satisfaction.

In conclusion, the affiliate marketing industry is evolving rapidly, and staying ahead of the curve is crucial for marketing professionals. By embracing influencer marketing, optimizing for mobile devices, leveraging video content, utilizing AI and automation, and delivering personalized experiences, affiliate marketers can adapt to the changing landscape and achieve marketing success.

Embracing Innovation for Continued Success

In the ever-evolving world of marketing, embracing innovation i crucial for continued success. This is particularly true in the niche c affiliate marketing, where staying ahead of the curve can make all th difference between thriving and falling behind. In this subchapter, w will explore how embracing innovation can propel your affiliat marketing efforts to new heights, helping you stay ahead of th competition and achieve long-term success.

One of the key aspects of embracing innovation is staying update with the latest trends and technological advancements. As an affiliat marketer, it is essential to constantly educate yourself about new tools platforms, and strategies that can enhance your marketing efforts. B keeping your finger on the pulse of the industry, you can identif emerging opportunities and leverage them to your advantage.

Innovation also involves thinking outside the box and being willing tc take risks. Rather than sticking to conventional marketing techniques successful affiliate marketers are those who dare to be different. The experiment with new approaches, explore unconventiona partnerships, and find unique ways to engage their target audience. By embracing innovation in your marketing campaigns, you can stanc out from the crowd and capture the attention of potential customers.

Furthermore, technology plays a crucial role in the success of affiliate marketing. Embracing innovative tools and platforms can streamline your processes, improve efficiency, and help you make data-driven decisions. From automation software that simplifies repetitive tasks tc advanced analytics tools that provide insights into consumer behavior, technology empowers affiliate marketers to optimize their strategies and achieve better results.

mbracing innovation is not just about adopting new technologies; it so requires a mindset shift. As a marketer, you must be open to hange and continuously seek opportunities for growth and nprovement. This could involve attending industry conferences, etworking with other marketers, and engaging in ongoing learning to xpand your knowledge and skills.

n conclusion, embracing innovation is essential for affiliate marketers vho seek continued success. By staying updated with the latest trends, ninking outside the box, leveraging technology, and adopting a rowth mindset, you can position yourself as a leader in the field of ffiliate marketing. Embrace innovation, and unlock the potential to ake your marketing efforts to new heights.

Chapter 11: Conclusion and Action Steps

Recap of Key Affiliate Marketing Strategies

In the world of marketing, affiliate marketing has emerged as powerful tool for businesses to expand their reach and boost sales. A an affiliate marketer, understanding and implementing effectiv strategies is crucial for success in this rapidly evolving field. In thi subchapter, we will recap some of the key affiliate marketing strategie that can help you unlock the full potential of this marketing technique

One of the fundamental strategies in affiliate marketing is choosing th right niche. By identifying a niche that aligns with your interests an expertise, you increase the chances of effectively promoting product or services and connecting with your target audience. A niche-focuse approach allows you to establish yourself as an authority in that are and build trust with your customers.

Building a strong online presence is another critical strategy in affiliat marketing. Creating a website or blog provides a platform to showcas your expertise and market relevant products or services. B consistently producing high-quality content, you can attract organi traffic and engage with potential customers. Additionally, leveragin the power of social media platforms, such as Facebook, Instagram, anc YouTube, can significantly amplify your reach and drive more traffi to your affiliate links.

Understanding the importance of SEO (Search Engine Optimization is essential for any affiliate marketer. By optimizing your website anc content for search engines, you can improve your visibility in searcl results and attract organic traffic. This involves keyword research, on page optimization, and link building strategies. Implementing effective

SEO techniques will ensure that your content ranks higher on search engine result pages, increasing the likelihood of conversions.

Furthermore, building and nurturing an email list is an invaluable strategy in affiliate marketing. By capturing the email addresses of your website visitors, you can cultivate a direct line of communication with potential customers. Through targeted email campaigns, you can deliver valuable content, promote products, and drive conversions. Building a relationship with your subscribers allows you to establish trust and credibility, increasing the chances of successful affiliate partnerships.

Lastly, monitoring and analyzing data is crucial in affiliate marketing. By tracking key metrics such as click-through rates, conversion rates, and customer demographics, you can gain insights into the effectiveness of your marketing campaigns. This data-driven approach allows you to optimize your strategies, make informed decisions, and continually improve your affiliate marketing efforts.

In conclusion, affiliate marketing offers immense opportunities for marketers to drive sales and generate revenue. By implementing the key strategies discussed in this subchapter, you can navigate the world of affiliate marketing with confidence and unlock the secrets to marketing success. Remember, choosing the right niche, building a strong online presence, optimizing for search engines, building an email list, and analyzing data are all essential components of a successful affiliate marketing strategy.

Next Steps for Affiliate Marketing Success

Congratulations! By now, you have gained a solid understanding of the fundamentals of affiliate marketing. You have learned about the various strategies, tactics, and tools that successful affiliates employ to drive traffic and generate sales. But your journey doesn't end here. In this subchapter, we will discuss the next steps you can take to achieve even greater success in the world of affiliate marketing.

1.   Diversify   Your   Traffic   Sources
While you may have found success with a particular traffic source, it is crucial to diversify and explore other avenues as well. This will not only help you reach a wider audience but also protect your business from potential risks associated with relying solely on one traffic source. Explore social media platforms, search engine optimization, email marketing, and paid advertising to expand your reach.

2.   Build   a   Strong   Brand:
Invest time and effort in building a strong brand identity. A recognizable and trustworthy brand will help you stand out from the competition and establish a loyal customer base. Create a professional website, design a compelling logo, and consistently provide valuable content to your audience. Focus on building relationships and trust with your customers to enhance your reputation within the niche.

3.   Continuously   Test   and   Optimize:
One of the key aspects of affiliate marketing is testing and optimization. Keep experimenting with different strategies, offers, landing pages, and ad creatives to identify what works best for your audience. Use data and analytics to measure the performance of your campaigns and make informed decisions. Continuously optimize your marketing efforts to maximize your conversions and revenue.

. Stay Updated with Industry Trends: Affiliate marketing is a dynamic industry that is constantly evolving. Stay updated with the latest trends, technologies, and best practices to maintain a competitive edge. Follow industry blogs, attend conferences, and join relevant communities to stay connected with fellow marketers and learn from their experiences. Adapt to changes swiftly and embrace new opportunities as they arise.

. Nurture Relationships with Partners: Building strong relationships with your affiliate partners is crucial for long-term success. Communicate regularly, provide support, and offer incentives to motivate your partners to promote your products or services. Collaborate with them to develop unique campaigns or joint ventures that can drive mutual success.

Remember, affiliate marketing is not a get-rich-quick scheme. It requires consistent effort, dedication, and a willingness to adapt. By implementing these next steps, you will be well on your way to achieving affiliate marketing success. Continue learning, experimenting, and refining your strategies, and soon enough, you will crack the code to become a highly successful affiliate marketer.

Final Thoughts and Encouragement for Marketing Triumph

Congratulations! You have come to the end of "Cracking the Affiliate Code: Insider Secrets for Marketing Success," and by doing so, you have taken a significant step towards achieving marketing triumph in the world of affiliate marketing. Throughout this book, you have gained valuable insights, strategies, and techniques that can propel your affiliate marketing journey to new heights. As we wrap up this subchapter, we would like to leave you with some final thoughts and words of encouragement to inspire you on your path to success.

First and foremost, remember that success in affiliate marketing is not an overnight phenomenon. It requires dedication, persistence, and continuous learning. The journey may have its ups and downs, but it's important to stay focused and committed to your goals. Keep honing your skills, experimenting with different strategies, and adapting to the ever-evolving landscape of digital marketing.

As you implement the insider secrets shared in this book, keep in mind that building strong relationships is key. Affiliate marketing is all about collaboration and cooperation. Network with fellow marketers, form partnerships, and leverage the power of collective knowledge. By nurturing these relationships, you can gain invaluable insights, access new opportunities, and establish yourself as a credible authority within your niche.

Embrace innovation and stay updated with the latest trends in marketing. The digital world is constantly evolving, and what works today may not work tomorrow. Stay ahead of the curve by investing time in research, attending industry conferences, and leveraging cutting-edge tools and technologies. Be open to trying new approaches and be willing to adapt your strategies accordingly.

emember, success in affiliate marketing is not solely measured by monetary gains. It's about building a sustainable business, creating value for your audience, and making a positive impact in your niche. Focus on providing quality content, addressing the needs and pain points of your target audience, and delivering exceptional customer experiences. By doing so, you will cultivate a loyal following and establish yourself as a trusted resource.

In conclusion, "Cracking the Affiliate Code: Insider Secrets for Marketing Success" has equipped you with the knowledge and tools to excel in the world of affiliate marketing. As you embark on your journey, remember to stay dedicated, build relationships, embrace innovation, and prioritize value creation. Marketing triumph is within your reach, and by implementing the strategies outlined in this book, you have set yourself on a path towards achieving it. The road may be challenging, but with persistence and determination, you have the power to unlock unprecedented success in affiliate marketing. Good luck!

Milton Keynes UK
Ingram Content Group UK Ltd.
UKHW020930231123
433129UK00016B/851